LET'S READ A
BOOK

WRITTEN & ILLUSTRATED BY
RUTH WALTON

SEA-TO-SEA
Mankato Collingwood London

Do you like reading books?

The great thing about books is that you can read them just about anywhere!

You can read outside, inside, on the sofa, in the park, on the train, in bed, or even on a plane.

Where is your favorite place to read?

When you want to read a new book, it's good to go to the library.

The librarians arrange books so that it is easy to find the kind of book you want.

FICTION

The **fiction** section is full of storybooks, arranged by the name of the **author**.

B

D

ALL ABOUT RABBITS

There are hundreds of different books in every library, so you can always find something exciting to read!

Librarian

Fact books are kept in the **nonfiction** section, so if you want to find out about something, this is a good place to look. Nonfiction books are arranged by subject.

NONFICTION

CRAFTS

COOKBOOKS

SCIENCE

GEOGRAPHY

ANIMALS

What is your favorite book?

All over the world, people love to read books. This book is written in the English **language,** but in different places, people speak other languages and use different **scripts** to write them.

How many different scripts can you see?

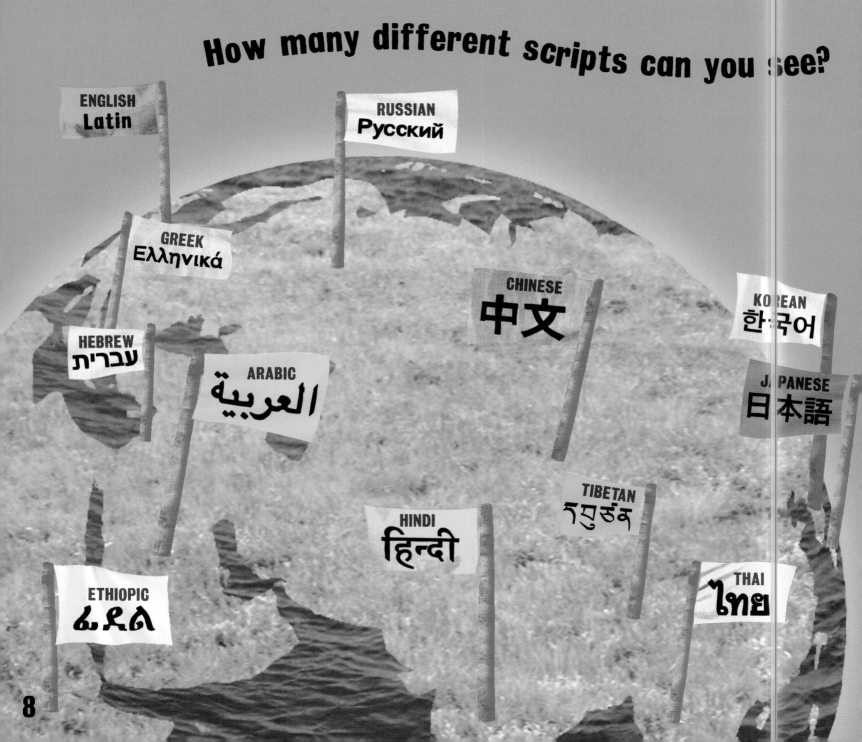

ENGLISH
Latin

RUSSIAN
Русский

GREEK
Ελληνικά

CHINESE
中文

KOREAN
한국어

HEBREW
עברית

ARABIC
العربية

JAPANESE
日本語

HINDI
हिन्दी

TIBETAN
དབུ་ཅན

ETHIOPIC
ፊደል

THAI
ไทย

Braille is a kind of writing used by blind and *visually impaired* people. It was invented in 1824 by Louis Braille, who was himself blind, when he was only 15. The letters are made of dots, which are raised up so that people can feel them with their fingertips.

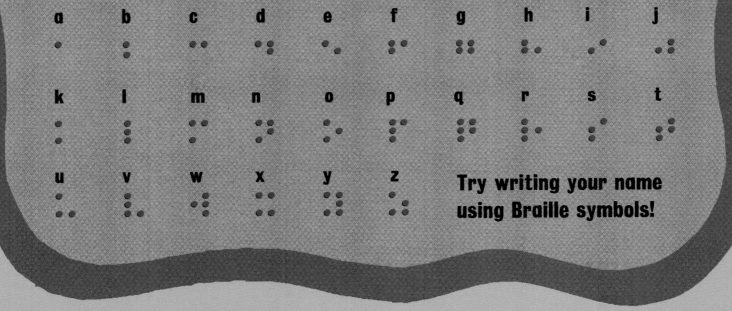

Try writing your name using Braille symbols!

The script that the English language is written in is called **Latin**. There are many more scripts that people use in different **cultures** around the world. In the past, people used different scripts, too.

When do you think writing was invented?

BOOKS and WRITING TIME LINE

3000 B.C.E.

The oldest writing known to humans is called **cuneiform**, and was written by pressing sticks into wet clay. It was used by the **Sumerian** people.

3000-2000 B.C.E.

Ancient Egyptians had three systems of writing called hieroglyphics, hieratics, and demotic. They were usually written on **papyrus.**

1500 B.C.E.

In China, writing was scratched onto bones and shells. The first books were made out of **bamboo** strips. This ancient writing is still in use and has hardly changed.

900 B.C.E.
The people of ancient Greece often wrote on pottery. Many of the letters in their alphabet are still in use today.

100 C.E.
The **Romans** wrote onto thin slices of wood or **scrolls** using the Latin alphabet.

500 C.E.
The first books were handwritten on **parchment**, and sewn together with string.

1400 C.E.
The **printing press** was invented and books became widely available for the first time ever!

How Are Books Made Now?

The person who writes the book is called the author. If the book needs pictures, they are made by an **illustrator** or a **photographer**.

An illustrator might use any of these things to make a picture.

How do you think the pictures in this book were made?

A **designer** arranges the words and pictures and shows the **editor,** who checks everything carefully to make sure there are no mistakes and makes an **index** for nonfiction books.

The designer uses a computer to arrange the words and pictures until they look just right!

The **publisher** arranges for the finished design to be printed on paper or made into an **e-book.**

Do you know what paper is made out of?

Most paper is made from wood, but it can be made from other **fibers,** too, including **hemp**, straw, and **cotton**.

It takes around 10 years for the tree to grow big enough to be cut down.

Where Do the Trees Grow?

*A lot of paper is made from trees grown in special **plantations**, but some is made from trees from old forests. Look for paper that has come from **sustainable** sources. This means the trees come from plantations that have been well cared for, and will be replaced when they are cut down.*

The trees are cut down and the branches are removed.
The logs and branches are taken away by trucks.

A worker who cuts down trees is called a lumberjack.

Log

Lumberjack

The wood is taken to a **paper mill** and turned into **pulp**.
This is sprayed onto a wire **mesh**. The sheet of pulp is
squeezed in a press to get some of the water out.

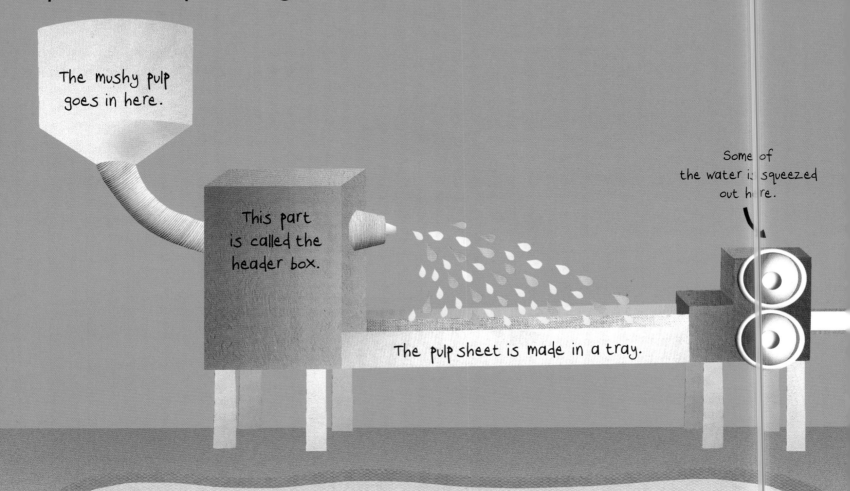

The mushy pulp goes in here.

This part is called the header box.

Some of the water is squeezed out here.

The pulp sheet is made in a tray.

How Is Pulp Made?

*Some paper mills use **chemicals** to break the wood down into pulp, a mushy mixture
of wood fibers and water. Others use machines to chop the wood into tiny pieces. Pulp
can also be made from old paper, which is collected and mixed with water until it turns
to mush. The ink is washed away using water and chemicals. In this way, paper can be
recycled up to six times before the fibers get too small to use!*

The sheet of pulp has started to look like paper. It travels through heated rollers to help it dry out. The paper is smoothed and rolled onto reels that look like giant rolls of toilet paper!

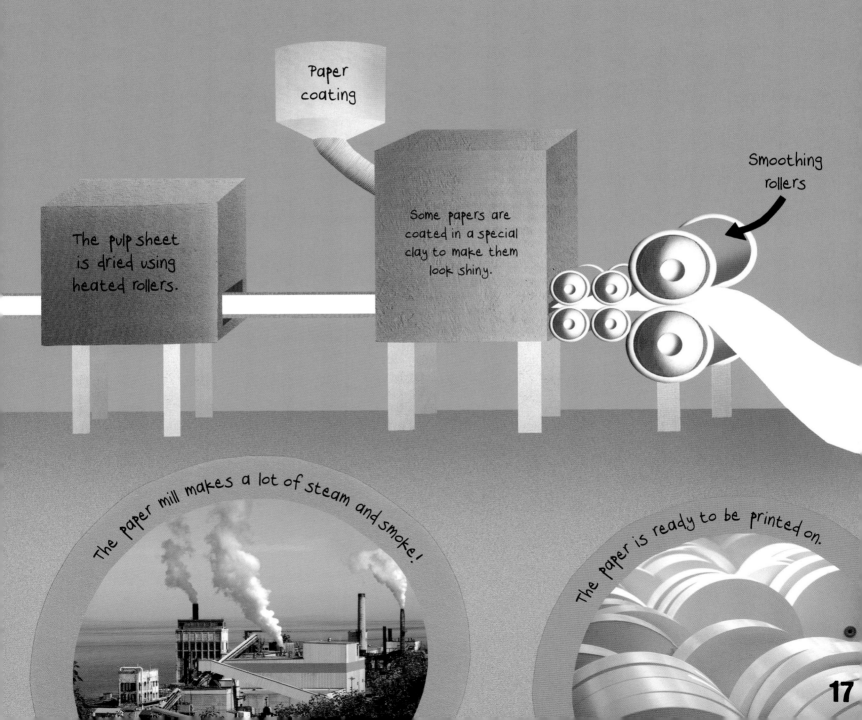

Paper coating

The pulp sheet is dried using heated rollers.

Some papers are coated in a special clay to make them look shiny.

Smoothing rollers

The paper mill makes a lot of steam and smoke!

The paper is ready to be printed on.

17

At the **printer**, the roll of paper is loaded into the printing press. Inside the press, it passes through many rollers.

Roll of paper

The paper travels through the press...

The rollers inside the printing press look like this.

Each roller has a **printing plate** on it that transfers the ink onto a special rubber sheet, which then transfers the ink onto the paper.

Each color of ink has its own roller.

Many pages can be printed onto one roll of paper. After the paper has been printed on, it passes over cold metal rollers that help the ink to dry. The prints are checked to make sure there are no mistakes!

This man is checking the printed pages.

... then the ink is dried inside here.

What Is Ink Made Out Of?

Most printing ink is made from oil mixed with pigments. Oil is a material that formed under the Earth's surface millions of years ago from dead plants and animals. Pigments are dry coloring materials. Ink can also be made using other kinds of oil, including oil made from **soybeans**!

How Does Color Printing Work?

Most books are printed using only four colors of ink: black, yellow, cyan, and magenta.

When the colors are printed on top of each other, they blend together to make different tones.

This is magenta.

This is yellow.

When magenta and cyan are printed on top of each other they make blue!

When yellow and magenta are printed on top of each other they make red!

When cyan and yellow are printed on top of each other, they make green!

This is cyan.

This is the cyan plate...

This is the black plate...

This is the yellow plate...

The colors in the picture are separated, and made into individual printing plates.

When they are put together they make a full color picture.

Here's the magenta plate...

...here are all the plates printed together!

Have you ever tried mixing paints to make new colors? What did you make?

21

How Is the Paper Made into a Book?

After the pages have been printed, they are **bound** together to turn them into a book. First the pages are put in the correct order and folded using a machine.

This is the folding machine.

This is the stitching machine.

Next, the pages are stitched together and trimmed using a **guillotine** paper trimmer.

The pages are joined to the cover using glue.

When the glue has dried, the book is finished and ready to read!

Take a look and find out what the
different parts of the book are called.

The cover of the
book is made from
mill board.

If you look at the center
of the pages of this book, you
can see the stitching that
holds it together!

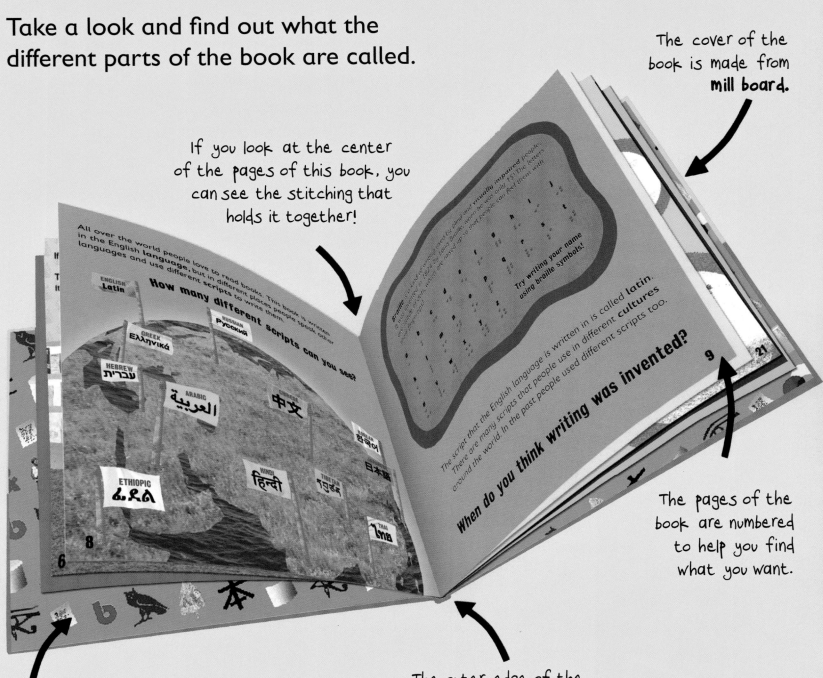

How many different scripts can you see?

ENGLISH
Latin

GREEK
Ελληνικά

RUSSIAN
Русский

HEBREW
עברית

ARABIC
العربية

中文

한국어

ETHIOPIC
ፊደል

HINDI
हिन्दी

TIBETAN
དབུ་ཅན

日本語

THAI
ไทย

The pages of the
book are numbered
to help you find
what you want.

The first and last
pages of the book are
called the **endpapers.**

The outer edge of the
center is called the spine.

What happens to the book next?

The books are packed into boxes and taken all around the world to the places where they will be read.

BOOKS direct

SCHOOL

Where could you find books in this picture?

THE CHEESE BOARD

EX LIBRIS BOOKSHOP

LIBRARY

Make your own book!

What you will need:

Pencil

Scissors

Small piece of thin cardboard
(half a cereal box)

4 sheets of letter paper
(used on one side)

Hole punch

12-inch (30-cm) piece of string
or ribbon

Step 2:

On the cardboard, draw around one of
the folded pieces of paper twice, and
cut them out.

Punch two holes in the
short side of each piece
of cardboard.

Step 1:

Fold a sheet of paper in half down
the longest side, so that any writing
is hidden inside!

Now fold it in half again.
Press the folds carefully.

Repeat with all four pieces of paper.

Step 3:

Punch holes in the folded side of each piece of paper, and stack them all on top of each other.

Put a piece of cardboard on the top and bottom of the pile.

Step 4:

Line up the holes and carefully thread the string or ribbon into one and out of the other.

Step 5:

Tie the ends together with a double bow, just like you tie your shoelaces!

Your book is finished!

What are you going to write in it?

Glossary

Author the writer of a book, play, or story

Bamboo a tropical grass plant that has hard woody stems

Bound tied or fastened together

Braille a kind of raised writing used by blind and visually impaired people

Chemical a substance produced by chemistry (the study of how things change when they are mixed together)

Cotton a natural fiber made from the seed pods of the cotton plant

Culture the language, customs, ideas, and art of a particular group of people

Cuneiform an ancient kind of writing

Designer person who makes the design of a book

E-book a digital book

Editor person who reads and corrects pieces of writing, before they are published

Endpaper the first and last pages of a book, which are glued to the cover

Fiber a long thin part of a plant, animal, or mineral

Fiction a made-up story

Guillotine a machine for cutting paper

Hemp a fast-growing plant used to make paper or cloth

Illustrator a person who makes pictures for books

Index a list at the back of a book with page numbers showing where each thing on the list appears

Language a system of spoken and written words

Latin the alphabet and language of the ancient Romans. Their alphabet is still used today

Mesh a wire screen with small spaces

Millboard a type of thick cardboard

Nonfiction a book of facts

Paper mill a factory where paper is made

Papyrus a plant in Egypt that was used as a material to write on

Parchment a thin sheet of animal skin used for writing on

Photographer a person who takes photographs

Plantation an area of land used for growing crops

Printer a company whose business is the printing of books, newspapers, or magazines

Printing plate thin sheet used in a printing press

Printing press a machine to transfer ink onto paper

Publisher a company that arranges for books to be made and sold

Pulp a soft wet material

Recycled processed to allow reuse

Romans the people of ancient Rome

Script the symbols used in writing

Scroll a roll of parchment

Soybeans beans from a soy plant

Sumerian people from the ancient culture of Sumer, now modern-day Iraq

Sustainable a way of managing resources so they will not run out

Visually impaired a person who cannot see very well, or not at all

29

Index

This edition first published in 2013 by
Sea-to-Sea Publications
Distributed by Black Rabbit Books
P.O. Box 3263, Mankato,
Minnesota 56002

Text and illustrations copyright
© Ruth Walton 2009, 2013

Printed in the United States of
America, North Mankato, MN.

9 8 7 6 5 4 3 2

Published by arrangement with the
Watts Publishing Group Ltd., London.

Library of Congress Cataloging-in-Publication Data

Walton, Ruth.
Let's read a book / written & illustrated by Ruth Walton.
    pages cm. -- (Let's find out)
Includes index.
Summary: "Briefly discusses the history of the printed
word and details how books are published today, from
the author's idea to editing and design, 4-color printing,
and distribution"--Provided by publisher.
ISBN 978-1-59771-387-0 (alk. paper)
1. Books--Juvenile literature. 2. Books and reading-
-Juvenile literature. 3. Book industries and trade--
Juvenile literature. 4. Publishers and publishing--Juvenile
literature. 5. Printing--Juvenile literature. 6. Writing--
History--Juvenile literature. I. Title.
Z116.A2W35 2013
002--dc23
                                    2011052693

Series Editor: Sarah Peutrill
Art Director: Jonathan Hair
Photographs: Ruth Walton, unless otherwise credited

Picture credits: I Stock Photo: 17bl (Dave Logan), 22t
(Jello5700), 22b (Kenneth Sponsler). Shutterstock: 17br
(Jim Lipschutz) 18b (Vasily Smirnov). Every attempt
has been made to clear copyright. Should there be any
inadvertent omission please apply to the publisher for
rectification.

RD/6000006415/001
May 2012

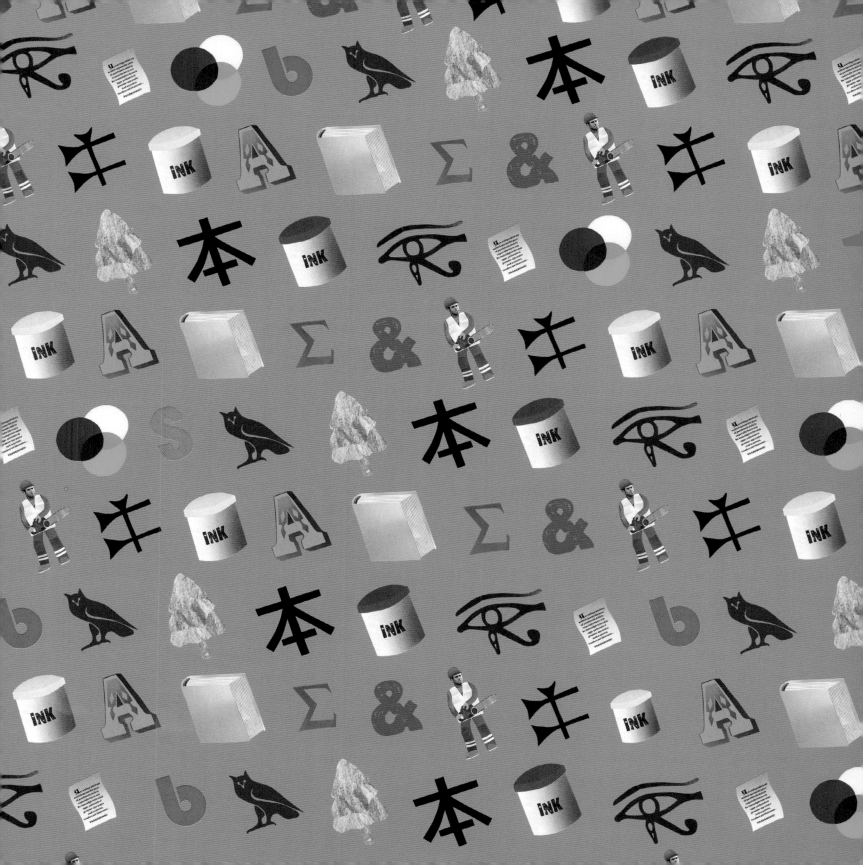